Warne's Transport Library

American Cars of the Seventies

Albert R. Bochroch

FREDERICK WARNE

Published by Frederick Warne (Publishers) Ltd London 1982

Also in Warne's Transport Library

Farm Tractors by Nick Baldwin
Trucks of the Sixties and Seventies by Nick Baldwin
American Trucks of the Seventies by Elliott Kahn
The Jeep by J-G Jeudy and Marc Tararine

ISBN 0 7232 2870 1

Filmset and printed in Great Britain by
BAS Printers Limited, Over Wallop, Hampshire

FOREWORD

The chances are that the 1970s will turn out to be the most difficult 10 years in the history of the American automobile business.

The decade opened with General Motors suffering a 65-day strike that contributed to an 8-year low in domestic sales. It closed with America's big 4—General Motors, Ford, Chrysler and American Motors—reeling under the impact of drastically reduced volume and with the once mighty Chrysler requiring government assistance to remain in business.

Import sales in 1969 amounted to 1,061,617 cars. Ten years later import registrations, of which close to 90 percent were from Japan, accounted for 2,339,004 units or 23 percent of total 1979 US new car sales.

Although the automotive industry is responsible for 18 percent of America's Gross National Product and provides employment for one out of every five of the nation's workforce, for much of the 1970s it was obliged to work with an, apparently, hostile US Department of Transportation.

Cheap fuel, as much a part of the American scene as Mom and apple pie, vanished during the 1970s. Ironically, although Americans still pay considerably less for gasoline than Common Market motorists, US drivers are the eventual losers as the higher prices charged in Europe are almost entirely due to higher taxes which are used to benefit the public while helping to reduce the consumption of fuel. Without taxes, the difference in basic fuel costs between America and Europe is a matter of pence.

Although Detroit may have been guilty of wishful thinking or, depending on your viewpoint, poor judgement, it did receive confusing signals during the 1970s. Even after the gasoline shortages of 1973–74, both dealer feedback and market research continued to indicate the American motorist's preference for larger cars. Detroit is reported to average $400 profit on smaller cars as against $1000 for larger models, and this may have contributed to its reluctance to embrace contemporary motorcars.

The decade that opened with soaring sales for garishly painted, giant tired, V8-powered vans, ended with the spotlight on front-wheel-drive, 4-cylinder engines, diesels and turbochargers.

ACKNOWLEDGEMENTS

The author would like to thank Louis Helverson, Librarian in Charge of the Automotive Collection of the Free Library of Philadelphia, for his generous assistance and for reading the manuscript. The author is indebted also to Tom Collins of Crain Publications and to Bob Fendell for their valuable suggestions, and to Alison Stooker of Ford, William B. Winters of General Motors, Bernard Mullens of Chrysler and to American Motors' Steven Harris for their cooperation.

Sales figures used throughout the book are based on R. L. Polk & Co statistical reports as they appear in *Automotive News Market Data Book*. Based on calendar year new car registrations, R. L. Polk figures differ slightly from manufacturers' production figures, dealer sales figures and annual model sales. Prices quoted are rounded-off and may not include freight, dealer preparation or local taxes.

GLOSSARY

American gallon = 3·7853 litres, approximately $\frac{4}{5}$ of an Imperial gallon

US	UK
automobile or motorcar	motorcar
bumper	fender
carburetor	carburettor
displacement capacity (cubic centimetres, cc's)	capacity (cubic inch displacement, CID, and cubic centimetres, cc's)
fender	wing
gasoline or fuel	petrol or fuel
hood	bonnet
sedan	saloon
shock absorber	dampers
station or estate wagon	estate wagon
tire	tyre
trunk	boot
windshield	windscreen

subcompact car	— less than 101-inch wheelbase
compact car	— 102 to 111-inch wheelbase
intermediate car	— 112 to 120-inch wheelbase
standard car	— greater than 120-inch wheelbase

1970

New car registrations in 1970 fell to 8,388,204, an 11 percent decrease over 1969. Gaining for the 9th consecutive year, imports accounted for 1,230,961 vehicles, 14·7 percent of the US total.

A strike cost General Motors 65 days, its share of the market dropping to 39·8 percent. Ford captured 26·4, a 2 percent increase over 1969. American Motors and Chrysler also benefited from GM's shutdown, AMC acquiring 3 percent of the market, up from 2·6 in 1969, with Chrysler reaching 16·1—a one percent gain.

The subcompact car (less than 101-inch wheelbase) entered the US scene in April, 1969, when American Motors introduced the Gremlin. Six months later Ford brought out the Pinto and GM, the Vega.

In 1970, four models, out of an industry total of 375, sold for less than $2000, and all but 24 models were priced under $5000.

GENERAL MOTORS

Chevrolet Monte Carlo   Chevy's intermediate size, 116-inch wheelbase, Monte Carlo coupe accommodated 5 passengers. Available with a 5700cc (350CID) V8 and 3-speed manual transmission, 6600cc (400CID) and 7400cc (454CID) V8s with automatic transmissions were popular options. Offered as a 2-door only, Monte Carlos were priced from $3200.

Chevrolet Chevelle SS 396   Completely restyled for 1970, a 4100cc (250CID) 6 and 3-speed manual transmission were 1970 Chevelle standards. Options included 5000cc (307CID) and 6600cc (400CID) V8s, automatic transmission, power front discs and, on the SS 396 only, a cowl induction hood. Offered as 4-door sedans, 2-door and 4-door hardtops and a convertible, over 400,000 of the $2700, and up, Chevelle/Malibu line were sold in 1970.

Pontiac Catalina   Standard for 1970 Catalina 4-door sedans and hardtops were 5700cc (350CID) V8s. Catalina convertibles, station wagons and Executive models came equipped with 6600cc (400CID) V8s. Priced from $3200, the 122-inch wheelbase Catalina and 125-inch wheelbase—224 inches overall—Executive were among the largest Pontiacs. The 164,650 Catalinas sold in 1970 represented 56,000 fewer than in 1969.

Pontiac Grand Prix   Distinguished by a new grille and the industry's longest hood, Pontiac's 1970 Grand Prix was offered only as a 2-door hardtop. Heavy duty 3-speed manual transmissions and 6600cc (400CID) V8s were standard, the 7400cc (450CID) V8 being a $58 option. Priced from $4100, 50,329 of Pontiac's 118-inch wheelbase coupe were sold in 1970.

Oldsmobile 98 Holiday Coupe   A 7400cc (455CID) 4-barrel Rocket V8, automatic transmission, power steering, power brakes, power windows and power seats were standard on the big 127-inch wheelbase, 225-inch overall, Olds 98. Also offered as a 4-door sedan, 4-door hardtop and a convertible, 62,566 of the big Olds were sold in 1970.

Oldsmobile Cutlass Supreme   Consisting of eight models, the Cutlass Six—2-door coupe, 4-door sedan, 2-door hardtop, 4-door hardtop and 2-seat wagon—and the Cutlass Supreme 2-door and 4-door hardtops and a convertible, the entire 1970 Cutlass line was designed to run on regular fuel. A 4100cc (250CID) 6 and 3-speed manual transmission were standard for Cutlass models, the Supreme series coming with 7400cc (455CID) V8s. All 2-door models were on 112-inch wheelbases, 4-door models using the 116-inch wheelbase.

Buick Riviera   A longer hood, wider rear windows and an improved 3-speed automatic transmission enhanced Buick's popular 2-door model in 1970. It was available only as a 119-inch wheelbase coupe, and a 7400cc (455CID) V8, dual exhausts, automatic transmission, power brakes and power steering were standard. Priced from $4900, 24,862 Rivieras were sold in 1970.

FORD MOTOR COMPANY

Buick Electra   Electra 225 Custom hardtops were Buick's top-of-the-line model in 1970. In addition to a 7400cc (455CID) V8, power steering and power brakes, a new engine-cooling system and all-new front suspension were standard. Offered in seven models, 104,152 of the big 127-inch wheelbase Electras were sold in 1970.

Mustang Cobra   Widely acclaimed when introduced in 1966, Ford's pony car was offered in a variety of models with engines ranging from a mild 3300cc (200CID) 6 to 7200cc (428CID) V8s. Shown is the fierce Cobra Jet with 'shaker' hood scoop, close-ratio 4-speed transmission with Hurst shifter and adjustable rear spoiler. Down 100,000 from 1969, total Mustang sales in 1970 were 162,711.

Cadillac Fleetwood   Most elegant of 1970 Cadillacs, the Fleetwood Brougham sported a new grille and padded vinyl roof with special moulding and cornering lights. A 375 HP, 7700cc (472CID) V8, automatic transmission, air conditioning and a host of power assists were Fleetwood standards. Over 10,000 of these enormous, 133-inch wheelbase, 4978 lb, $7300 sedans were purchased in 1970.

Torino Brougham   New in 1970, Ford's Torino soon established itself as a favourite with buyers of mid-size cars. Priced from $2700, 305,277 Torinos were bought during its first year. The 2-door hardtop shown here was one of 14 Torino models sharing a 117-inch wheelbase. Engines ranged from a 4100cc (250CID) 6 to a 7000cc (429CID) V8.

Ford Custom 500 Sedan Priced from $2900, the Custom 500 was Ford's lowest priced, standard size, 4-door sedan. Available in 19 body styles with an economy-minded 4000cc (240CID) 6 and 3-speed manual transmission as standard, optional V8s and automatic transmissions were specified by almost 100 percent of those buying the big Ford.

Continental Mark III Top of the Ford Motor Company line in 1970 was the lavishly appointed Lincoln Continental Mark III coupe. A 7600cc (465CID) V8, power brakes, power steering, power windows and power seats, Michelin tires, concealed headlights, walnut veneers and interior decor by Cartier were standard. At 117 inches, the Mark III wheelbase was 10 inches less than that of the Continental sedan. However, its weight, 4900 lb, was about the same. 56,654 Lincolns were sold in 1970.

CHRYSLER CORPORATION

Mercury Cyclone Spoiler The Lincoln-Mercury Division's muscle car, this brawny 117-inch wheelbase Cyclone Spoiler, was powered by a 370 HP, 7000cc (429CID) V8 with Ram Air Induction. Available only as a hardtop coupe, the Cyclone competition package included a Hurst shifter, front anti-lift spoiler, rear deck air-foil and 8000 RPM tachometer.

Plymouth Valiant Duster Plymouth's Duster was delivered with a new 3200cc (198CID) 6 or optional V8s of 5200cc (318CID) and 5600cc (340CID). Also introduced in 1970 was a new Duster grille and increased fuel tank protection. Total Valiant sales reached 246,013 in 1970.

Dodge Custom Camper Special Reflecting America's interest in outdoor life, 1970 sales of recreational vehicles—vans, campers, 4-wheel-drives and light trucks—slowed less than the sale of passenger cars. Sold with a 3700cc (225CID) 6 or 5200cc (318CID) and 5900cc (360CID) V8s, 1970 Dodge D-200s handled slide-on campers of up to 10·5 feet and, with its 128-inch wheelbase, carried loads of 3100 lb.

New in 1970 and available with either 6 cylinder or V8 engines was this Dodge Custom Sportsman Van.

Dodge Charger A popular speciality car of the late 1960s, the Charger began sharing its 117-inch wheelbase with the Dodge Coronet line during the 1970 model year. Although a 3700cc (225CID) 6 was the standard Charger engine, 99 percent of all Chargers sold during 1970 were equipped with V8 engines.

AMERICAN MOTORS

Hornet Sedan AMC added this 4-door model to its Hornet line in 1970. Standard for the 108-inch wheelbase compact 2-door and 4-door sedans was a 3300cc (199CID) 6. A larger 3800cc (232CID) 6 and 5000cc (304CID) V8 were options. Priced from $2000, 84,000 Hornets were sold in 1970.

Ambassador SST All seven models of AMC's top-of-the-line 1970 Ambassador series featured new rear-end styling. Standard equipment for six of the seven models included a 5000cc (304CID) V8, automatic transmission and air conditioning. Priced from $3100, AMC sold 56,033 Ambassadors in 1970.

1971

Americans bought 9,830,266 new motorcars in 1971, a 16 percent increase over 1970 and a record high in annual sales.

Import sales of 1,465,673 units represented 15·06 percent of the 1971 total, the 10th consecutive year imports registered an increased share of the US market.

General Motors' share of the market rose to 45·16 percent. Ford, Chrysler and American Motors reported modest losses.

Of the 298 models offered by Detroit's Big 4, there were 7 subcompacts, 23 compacts, 81 intermediates, 156 standards and 31 specialty cars.

Phasing-out began on high-test fuels, the majority of new models accepting low lead or no lead gasoline.

GENERAL MOTORS

Chevrolet Vega Few new cars were as eagerly awaited as GM's Vega. Starting with a clean sheet, Chevrolet engineers developed an innovative 2300cc (140CID) sleeveless aluminum overhead cam 4 with a 3-speed manual transmission and an advanced suspension. Available on a 97-inch wheelbase were a station wagon, hatchback coupe, 2-door sedan and small truck. Priced from $2100, 323,443 Vegas were bought in 1971.

Chevrolet Nova Rally Coupe Offered as 2-door coupes and 4-door sedans, standard for Chevrolet's compact Nova was a 4100cc (250CID) 6 featuring GM's new exhaust emission control and a 3-speed manual transmission. Priced from $2400, Chevrolet's 6000 dealers sold 235,553 Novas in 1971.

Pontiac Grand Ville Leading the Pontiac parade in 1971 was the big, 126-inch wheelbase, Grand Ville. It was available as a 2-door hardtop, convertible or 4-door as illustrated. Priced from $4300, standard features are a regular-fuel burning 7400cc (455CID) V8 engine, 3-speed manual transmission, power steering and power brakes. Automatic transmissions were a popular $243 option.

Chevrolet Caprice Chevrolet's best seller in 1971, the Caprice/Impala line, featured fresh styling and a completely new chassis with full coil suspension. Available in 2-door and 4-door sedans, a 6600cc (400CID) V8 and 3-speed manual transmission were standard on the big 125-inch wheelbase, $3800 Caprice.

Pontiac GTO Sporting a new front end, new hood, and powered by a 6600cc (400CID) 4-barrel V8 linked to a heavy-duty, 3-speed manual transmission, the 112-inch wheelbase GTO was Pontiac's entry in the 'muscle car' sweepstakes. Also available was a GTO convertible and, as options, a 7400cc (455CID) V8 and, for $195, a 4-speed manual transmission.

Oldsmobile Toronado   Introduced in 1966, the front-wheel-drive Toronado was a rarity among American automobiles. Stretched 3 inches to a 122-inch wheelbase in 1971, standard equipment included power steering, power front disc brakes, automatic transmission and a 7400cc (455CID) V8. Available only as a 2-door hardtop, 38,721 of the $5500 Toronado were sold in 1971.

Buick LeSabre   Available as 4-door sedans, 2-door and 4-door hardtops and as a convertible, with a 5700cc (350CID) V8; 3-speed manual transmission and front disc brakes were standard equipment on the 124-inch wheelbase LeSabre. Priced from $3800, 176,731 LeSabres were sold in 1971.

FORD MOTOR COMPANY

Cadillac Sedan de Ville and Eldorado Convertible   Cadillac's most popular model, the 130-inch wheelbase Sedan de Ville, was equipped with a 7500cc (472CID) V8, automatic transmission, power steering, power disc brakes and power windows. Priced from $6400, 1971 Sedan de Ville sales were 180,332.

Powered by an 8200cc (500CID) V8, the largest production engine of its time, the all-new front-wheel-drive Eldorado featured an inward folding top that permitted full-width rear seating. 35,613 of the $7400, and up, luxury convertibles were bought in 1971.

Ford Pinto   Priced just under $2000, and originally available only in coupe form, the Pinto was equipped with rack and pinion steering, a relatively uncommon feature for America at the time. Standard for the 94·2-inch subcompact was a 1600cc (98CID) 4 and 3-speed manual transmission. A 2000cc (122CID) 4, automatic transmission and a variety of trims became options. Ford dealers sold over 328,000 Pintos in 1971, its first full year.

CHRYSLER CORPORATION

Ford Maverick Grabber Introduced in April, 1969, Ford's compact Maverick came as 2-door and 4-door sedans plus the sporty 2-door Grabber. Standard was a 2800cc (170CID) 6 and 3-speed manual transmission. 1971 Maverick sales dropped to 247,626 from 342,198 the previous year.

Plymouth Sport Fury The 1971 Plymouth Sport Fury 2-door hardtop was one of 25 models in five Fury lines. Automatic transmission and a 5200cc (318CID) V8 were standard on the 120-inch wheelbase, intermediate size coupe. Priced from $3400, over 300,000 Furys were sold in 1971.

Lincoln/Mercury Marquis Brougham The 1971 Marquis Brougham had several features not usually found as standard equipment on medium-priced, $3800 and up, sedans. Delivered with a 7000cc (429CID) V8, automatic transmission, power windows, power steering, power brakes, concealed headlights and doors containing safety-steel guard rails, the big, 124-inch wheelbase, Marquis was available as a 4-door sedan, 2-door hardtop and 4-door hardtop.

Chrysler LeBaron Flagship of Chrysler's 1971 line was the Imperial LeBaron. Available as a 127-inch wheelbase 2-door hardtop and the 4-door hardtop shown here, a 6600cc (440CID) V8, designed to burn regular grade gasoline, was standard as were automatic transmission, power brakes and power steering. Priced from $6800, 12,018 Imperials were bought in 1971.

Dodge Dart One of the first US compacts, the 111-inch wheelbase Dart was introduced in 1963. Standard for the 1971 Dart was a 3200cc (198CID) 6 or optional 5200cc (318CID) V8. Priced from $2300, 1971 sales of 208,085 Darts made it the leading seller in the Dodge line.

AMERICAN MOTORS

AMC Matador Estate Wagon A 4-door sedan, 2-door hardtop and wagon completed AMC's new line of intermediates. Power for the 118-inch wheelbase Matador ranged from a 3800cc (232CID) 6 to AMC's new 6600cc (401CID) V8. Priced from $2800, over 45,000 Matadors were sold during 1971.

AMC Gremlin Standard for the 1971 AMC Gremlin, America's first subcompact, was a 3800cc (232CID) 6 with either floor or column-mounted 3-speed manual transmissions. A 4200cc (258CID) 6 and automatic transmission were optional. AMC's best-selling car, 70,096 of the $2000 fastbacks were bought in 1971.

AMC Javelin SST Newly designed for 1971, the Javelin sport coupe featured a boxed steel member welded inside each door as passenger protection against side impact. 1971 Javelin wheelbases were increased to 110 inches and the rear tread made 3 inches wider. Standard was a 3800cc (232CID) 6 and a 3-speed manual transmission. Options included AMC's new 6600cc (401CID) V8.

1972

The sale of 10,487,794 new cars in 1972 represented a 1·08 gain over 1971 with imports accounting for 1,465,673 of the total.

Although smaller US makes and imports earned larger shares of the market, America's biggest 1972 sellers were the largest Fords and Chevrolets, with sales of 794,438 and 906,541 respectively.

The V8 engine's share of the US new car market rose to 69·25 percent, almost 10 points, however, under its 1968 peak.

Noteworthy in 1972 were industry-wide steps to improve passenger safety, advances in emission control systems and the widespread use of engines accepting low lead or no lead fuel.

GENERAL MOTORS

Chevrolet Kingswood Wagon   The 4857-lb, 125-inch wheelbase Kingswood was the largest of seven wagons in the larger Chevrolet line. Costs ranged from the Brookwood's $3900 to $4500 for the Kingswood with its standard 6600cc (400CID) V8. Total Chevrolet Division wagon sales for 1972 were: 61,000 subcompact Vegas, 46,000 mid-size Chevelles and 159,000 full-size Chevrolets.

Chevrolet Malibu   One of six models in the intermediate-size Chevelle line, 1972 Malibu 2-door hardtops came with a 3200cc (250CID) 6 or 5000cc (307CID) V8 as standard equipment. Prices ranged from $2800 for the 6-cylinder 4-door to $3300 for the V8 convertible. Wheelbase for 2-door models was 112 inches, 116 for 4-doors and estate wagons.

Pontiac Grand Prix   A new grille, twin-level bumpers and a new headlight arrangement identified Pontiac's Grand Prix in 1972. Made only as a 2-door hardtop, as illustrated, a 6600cc (400CID) V8, automatic transmission, power brakes and power windows were standard. Priced at $4600, Pontiac sold 93,000 Grand Prix coupes in 1972.

Buick Electra   In 1972, the 4724-lb, 127-inch wheelbase Electra, largest and heaviest in the line, was Buick's best-selling model. Featuring a restyled hood, wider grille and improved bumpers, a 7400cc (455CID) V8, automatic transmission, power brakes and power steering were standard. Available as 2-door and 4-door hardtops, Electra prices began at $4800.

Oldsmobile Cutlass and Delta 88   The Cutlass (above) and Delta 88 (below) are two reasons that GM's Oldsmobile Division sold 691,000 cars in 1972, passing Pontiac and Buick to become General Motors' second largest selling nameplate. The Delta 88 Royal hardtop with a 124-inch wheelbase and 5700cc (350CID) V8, sold for $4200.

Selling from $3100 to $3500, the intermediate Cutlass 2-door was on a 112-inch wheelbase, the 4-door sedan, 116 inches.

Cadillac Calais   Available as 2-door and 4-door hardtops on a 130-inch wheelbase, standard was a 7500cc (472CID) V8, automatic transmission and a host of power equipment. At $6100 the 1972 Calais was Cadillac's lowest priced (and slowest selling) model. Silhouetted in the background is the graceful rear-window and trunk of an early Cadillac.

FORD MOTOR COMPANY

Ford Mustang   One of five Mustangs offered by Ford in 1972, the racy Mach I came equipped with a 5000cc (302CID) V8, functional hoodscoops, wide-oval tires and colour-keyed bumpers. Automatic or 4-speed manual transmissions were optional. Priced from $2800 to $3100, 108,756 of Ford's 109-inch wheelbased 'Pony cars' were sold in 1972.

Ford Thunderbird   Introduced in 1955 as a small 2-seater, Ford's all-new 1972 T-Bird put 4800 lb on a 120-inch wheelbase. Powered by a 6600cc (400CID) V8, the luxury coupe was equipped with Michelin steel-belted radials and a host of power assists. Close to 53,000 of the $5600 T-Birds were purchased in 1972.

Ford Torino   Ford's 1972 Torino line consisted of 9 models. Shown is the Grand Torino Sport, a 2-door hardtop with a 5000cc (302CID) V8 as standard. Optional were a 4100cc (250CID) 6 and five V8s of up to 7000cc (429CID). Priced from $2700 to $3500, 2-door Torino's had 114-inch wheelbases, 4 doors and wagons measuring 118 inches. Over 421,000 mid-size Torinos were bought in 1972.

Mercury Montego   New in 1972, the Montego MX 4-door Brougham was Lincoln-Mercury's entry in the growing intermediate field. Standard equipment included a 4100cc (250CID) 6, 3-speed column-mounted transmission, concealed windscreen wipers and front disc brakes. Priced from $2900 to $3400, nine models were offered in 1972.

AMERICAN MOTORS

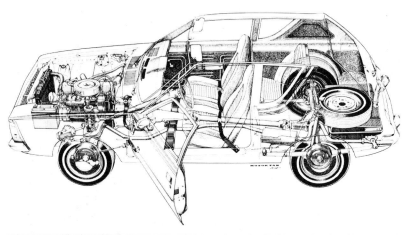

Cougar XR-7 Mercury called their 1972 Cougar XR-7 'the best equipped luxury sports car in the country'. We may question the Cougar as a sports car, but it was indeed well equipped. A 5700cc (351CID) V8, 3-speed floor shift, leather seats, woodgrain steering wheel, tachometer and twin racing mirrors were standard. Available in five models, the XR-7 sold for $3700.

Lincoln Continental Ford's 1972 flagship was this all-new Continental Mark IV, 2-door hardtop. Distinguished by a bolder grille and longer, lower hood, standard for the 5100 lb Mark IV was a 7400cc (460CID) V8, a full complement of power assists, air conditioning, automatic transmission, Michelin tires, woodgrained instrument panel and a Cartier timepiece. Lincoln sales in 1972 reached 90,000, of which the $9,000 Mark IV accounted for over half.

AMC Gremlin Offered as options on AMC's subcompact Gremlin was a 5000cc (304CID) V8, a new automatic transmission and sun roof. Continuing as standard on the 96-inch wheelbase, 4-passenger, 2-door was a 3800cc (232CID) 6 and 3-speed manual transmission. (The drawing shows fitting of Gremlin's new 'Torque-Command' transmission and 4-passenger seating arrangement.) Priced from $2100, more than 94,000 Gremlins were sold in 1972.

CHRYSLER CORPORATION

Plymouth Sebring 2-Door Hardtop   One of 11 models in Plymouth's intermediate size Satellite series, the Sebring 2-door, was on a 115-inch wheelbase while 4-door and wagon models used a wheelbase of 117·5 inches. Delivered with a 3700cc (225CID) 6, V8s from 5200cc (318CID) to 7400cc (440CID) and automatic transmissions were optional. Satellite sales reached 127,440 in 1972.

Hornet Sportabout   Created by famous Italian clothing designer, Aldo Gucci, the 'Gucci' Hornet Sportabout sedan-wagon featured boldly-striped green, red and buff seats and door panels. Also offered in 2-door and 4-door sedans, standard for the 108-inch wheelbase compact was AMC's 3800cc (232CID) 6 and 3-speed manual transmission. Automatic transmission, a 4200cc (258CID) 6 and two V8s were options.

Chrysler Newport Royal   Featuring unibody construction and torsion bar suspension, the full-size, 122-inch wheelbase, Chrysler Newport Royal 2-door hardtop was one of three Newport models. Standard was a 6600cc (400CID) V8 and automatic transmission; a 7400cc (450CID) V8 was optional. Priced from $4200, 1972 Newport sales reached 105,110.

Dodge Coronet Custom Sedan Featured in 1972 were all-new interior and exterior styling, including full-width front and rear bumpers as shown. Standard for the Coronet coupe and sedan was a 3700cc (225CID) 6, while Custom 4-door sedans and wagons were delivered with a 5200cc (318CID) V8. Priced from $2900, 146,929 of the intermediate Coronet line were sold in 1972.

1973

A record 11,350,995 new cars were bought by Americans in 1973. Accounting for 1,719,913 of the total, imports registered still another increase in US sales.

American car makers gained in both dollar volume and number of units sold. GM reported sales of 5,053,540 passenger cars; Ford 2,666,915; Chrysler 1,512,520 and American Motors 392,105.

Prices continued to rise, the majority of 1973 automobiles costing at least 10 percent more than comparable 1972 models.

The summer of 1973 witnessed the beginnings of the oil embargo induced 1973–74 fuel shortage. A period of long queues and short tempers, it signalled the start of new game plans that were to transform the American automobile industry.

Showing commendable precedence, in January 1973, six months before the oil embargo, GM began to redesign their entire line.

Dubbed 'downsizing', immediate objectives were to meet, or surpass, government mandated miles-per-gallon fuel averages and comply with Department of Transportation emission and safety standards.

All 1973 GM models featured new bumpers that met or exceeded Federal impact requirements; driver and front seat passenger shoulder belts; doors with horizontally welded steel guard beams and roofs with two steel safety panels.

As new models appeared, 'downsizing' successfully reduced the size and weight of GM cars without sacrificing passenger space.

Chevrolet Vega Offered in four models, hatchback and notchback coupes, a wagon and a small panel truck, Vegas captured the 1973 subcompact sweepstakes with sales of 452,654. However, persistent problems with the Vega's unique aluminum engine, a 2300cc (140CID) overhead cam 4, would lead to adopting an iron block 4 and, eventually, to dropping the Vega line.

Chevelle Laguna New to Chevrolet's intermediate-size Chevelle line were Laguna 2-door and 4-door hardtops and a 4-door wagon. Standard for the 112-inch wheelbase hardtop was a 5700cc (350CID) V8 and 3-speed manual transmission, the 116-inch wheelbase being standard for the wagon. 1973 Laguna prices ranged from $3100 to $3700.

Pontiac Grand Ville Restyled for 1973, the Grand Ville was offered as a 2-door and 4-door hardtop and convertible with a 7400cc (455CID) V8 and automatic transmission. Priced from $4400 to $4700, 60,006 of the big, 124-inch wheelbase, 4655-lb, top-of-the-line Pontiacs were sold in 1973.

Pontiac Ventura Hatchback Pontiac's new Ventura coupe featured a folding rear seat and spring-loaded rear hatchback panel. Also available in the 111-inch wheelbase Ventura series were a 2-door coupe, 4-door sedan and custom models with more elaborate trim. Standard was a 4100cc (250CID) 6 and 3-speed manual transmission. A 5700cc (350CID) V8 and 4-speed manual transmission were popular options.

Oldsmobile Regency 98 Added to Oldsmobile's 98 line in 1973 was the Regency, a new luxury sedan. Available as 2-door and 4-door sedans, a 7400cc (455CID) Rocket V8, automatic transmission, power brakes and power steering were standard. Priced from $4800, over 115,000 big 98s were sold in 1973.

Oldsmobile Omega Smallest and lightest of the fast-moving Oldsmobile line was the 111-inch wheelbase, 3300-lb Omega compact. Selling 808,889 of all models, 1973 Oldsmobiles were GM's second largest seller. Available in three models, a 4100cc (250CID) 6 and 3-speed manual transmissions were Omega standards.

Opel Manta Made at GM's Opel plant in Russelheim, West Germany, more than 2000 Buick dealers handled Opels in the US. With 1973 sales of 80,000, Opel's new Manta Luxus sports coupe joined 550,000 Opels already on American roads. Standard was a 1900cc (116CID) 4 with 4-speed manual transmission and power disc brakes. A sun roof and automatic transmission were available on some models.

Buick Regal The new intermediate-size 1973 Regal Colonnade hardtop, one of Buick's fast-selling Century Group, featured a formal roof line and rectangular rear quarter windows. Standard for the 112-inch wheelbase coupe was a 5700cc (350CID) V8 with manual transmission.

Cadillac Coupe de Ville A new grille, bumpers and hood, as well as improved suspension, shock absorbers and body mounts, were on all 1973 Cadillacs. With 1973 sales of 202,000, the $6300 Coupe de Ville was by far Cadillac's most popular model. Available as 2-door and 4-door hardtops, a 7500cc (472CID) V8, automatic transmission, power steering and power brakes were standard.

FORD MOTOR COMPANY

Pinto Runabout   With 1973 sales of 268,472 coupes and 212,634 wagons, Ford's $2500 Pinto thrived in the growing field of economy subcompacts. Standard features included a 1600cc (98CID) 4, fully synchronized 4-speed transmission and rack and pinion steering. A 2000cc (120CID) 4 and automatic transmission were options. The 3-door Runabout shown here featured an optional sun roof.

Lincoln-Mercury Marquis Brougham   All 13 full-size Mercury models were redesigned for 1973. Flagship of the line, the big, 124-inch, 4800-lb, 4-door hardtop Marquis Brougham was delivered with a 7400cc (460CID) V8 and automatic transmission. Priced from $4800 to $5400, 78,500 of the Marquis line were sold in 1973.

Mercury Capri   Made by Ford in West Germany, the Capri was sold in the US by over 1000 Lincoln-Mercury dealers. With 1973 sales over 115,000, the Capri was one of America's best-selling imports until slowed by rising German marks and falling dollars. Standard was a 2000cc (122CID) 4, with steel-belted radial tires, a 4-speed manual transmission and tachometer. Popular options for the 101-inch wheelbase sports coupe were a 2600cc (159CID) V6 and sliding sun roof.

Ford LTD Country Squire Always a strong part of the Ford line, estate wagons were represented by 11 models (six Ford, three Torino and two Pinto) in 1973. Ford's big 121-inch wheelbase, 4900-lb wagon featured a cargo capacity of 96·2 cubic feet and a 3-way 'Doorgate'. Standard was a 5700cc (351CID) V8, automatic transmission, power brakes, power steering and a power tailgate window.

Ford LTD 4-Door Hardtop Totally restyled for 1973, the LTD boasted a new grille, wraparound parking lights, side door steel guard rails and new energy absorbing bumpers. Other LTD models were a 2-door hardtop, 2-door Pillared hardtop, 2-door Brougham, 4-door Pillared hardtop and 4-door Brougham. Standard was a 5700cc (351CID) V8, automatic transmission, power steering and power front disc brakes. Optional engines included a 7400cc (460CID) V8.

CHRYSLER CORPORATION

Dodge 200 Club Cab Although sold as pickup trucks rated to haul payloads or trailers of up to 4950 lb on its 131-inch wheelbase, light trucks of this type became popular all-round vehicles with such diverse users as campers, housewives and students. Priced from $3500, engine availability ranged from a 3700cc (225CID) 6 to 7200cc (440CID) V8s.

Dodge Colt GT and Wagon Unlike captive imports, such as GM's Opel and the Ford Capri, Colts were made for Dodge in Japan by Mitsubishi. Offered as 2-door and 4-door sedans, a hardtop, GT coupe and wagon, the 2200-lb subcompact Colt was on a 95·3-inch wheelbase. Standard was a 1600cc (97·5CID) 4 with a 4-speed manual transmission. Chrysler's Dodge division sold 35,000 Colts in 1973.

Plymouth Cricket Wagon Made for Plymouth by Chrysler in England, where it was known as the Avenger, Crickets sold in America were 4-door sedans and estate wagons. Standard was a 1500cc (91·4CID) 4, power front disc brakes, rack and pinion steering and 4-speed manual transmission. US Cricket sales were discontinued following the 1973 model year.

AMERICAN MOTORS CORPORATION

AMC Gremlin Having marketed a Gucci-inspired Hornet, AMC turned to famed jeans maker Levi who styled a 1973 Country/Western Gremlin with interiors featuring orange stitching and copper rivets. Available in eight optional trims and three engines, the standard 3800cc (232CID) 6 and two V8s, sales of the 96-inch wheelbase, $2400 subcompact exceeded 133,000 in 1973.

AMC Ambassador Brougham Standard equipment on AMC's luxury Ambassador were such customary extras as air conditioning, radio, tinted glass, undercoating and power-assisted windows. AMC's 5700cc (360CID) V8 was standard, a 6600cc (401CID) V8 optional.

AMC Wagons American Motors' 1973 wagon line covered the compact Hornet Sportabout (bottom), intermediate Matador (centre) and luxury-size Ambassador (top). Engines for AMC's wagon train were the standard 3800cc (232CID) 6 and V8s of 5000cc (304CID), 5700cc (360CID) and 6600cc (401CID). Hornet 6 wagons were priced at $3000, the Matador at $3300 with the Ambassador V8 around $5000.

1974

American dealers sold 8,701,094 new motorcars in 1974: 2,649,901, 23·35 percent fewer than in 1973. Domestic makes accounted for 7,331,946 new car registrations while import sales represented 1,369,148 units, 15·74 percent of the American market.

American-made small cars, subcompacts and compacts, increased from 2,592,468 units in 1973 to 2,970,407 in 1974. For the first time in 12 years the percentage of new models sold with V8 engines dropped below 60 percent.

General Motors' share of new car sales fell to 41·89 percent. Ford's percentage rose slightly to 24·66, Chrysler remained around 13·50 and American Motors finished 1974 with a share of 3·79.

By mid-year the American automobile industry was committed to making smaller, more fuel-efficient cars, a step that had little effect on the gasoline lines of 1974.

GENERAL MOTORS

Retrospectively, 1974 was an interim year for GM's 'downsizing' program. Although activated in 1973, the long, 3 to 5 year lead time required to tool-up for new models was not evident as many GM cars appeared with added pounds and inches.

Pontiac Firebird   Restyled for 1974, the 108-inch wheelbase compact-size Trans Am featured an improved aerodynamic front-end. Star of the four model Firebird sports coupe line, the Trans Am's standard engine was a 7400cc (455CID) V8. Prices ranged from $3100 for the basic Firebird to $4300 for the Trans Am.

Chevrolet Monte Carlo S   Chevrolet's intermediate, 116-inch wheelbase Monte Carlo S was available only as a luxury 2-door Sports or Landau coupe. Standard was a 5700cc (350CID) V8, power brakes, power steering and radial tires. Priced from $3700, 285,000 of Chevrolet's 'personal' car were sold in 1974.

Pontiac Grand Prix   Pontiac's familiar split-centre front-end theme was carried a step further on the 1974 Grand Prix. Standard for Pontiac's top-of-the-line 2-door, the only model offered, was a 6600cc (400CID) V8. Priced from $4700, 1974 Grand Prix sales were 81,547, down sharply from 144,666 sold in 1973.

Oldsmobile Cutlass Supreme Hardtop 4-Door Sedan   A leading seller in the popular Oldsmobile line was the intermediate class Cutlass. Standard on all 11 Cutlass models in 1974 was a 5700cc (350CID) Rocket V8, automatic transmission and front disc power brakes.

Buick Apollo 4-Door Sedan   Built on GM's 111-inch wheelbase, the 1974 Apollo was Buick's entry in the fast-growing field of compact motorcars. Available as a hatchback, 2-door coupe and 4-door sedan, a 4100cc (250CID) 6 and 3-speed manual transmission were standard.

Oldsmobile Omega Coupe   All three models of the compact Omega were built on 111-inch wheelbases. New in 1974 was the 'S' sports package that included special rally suspension and super-stock wheels. Priced from $2800 with the standard 4100cc (250CID) 6, a 5700cc (350CID) V8 was available for an added $164.

Buick Riviera   A squared-off rear deck lid and new rear side windows were featured by Buick's smartly styled 1974 Riviera. Offered only as a coupe, standard for the big, 122-inch wheelbase, 4680-lb luxury 2-door was a 7400cc (455CID) V8 and automatic transmission. Priced from $5400, 1974 sales of 18,310 were almost 10,000 fewer than in 1973.

FORD MOTOR COMPANY

Cadillac Fleetwood Sixty Special Brougham Except for Cadillac limousines, the 133-inch wheelbase, 233·7 inches overall, 5388-lb Fleetwood Sixty Special Brougham was the largest and heaviest 1974 production motorcar made in America. Sold only as a 4-door sedan, the 1974 Fleetwood Brougham featured a redesigned front end, new grille and new lighting arrangement. Standard was a 7500cc (472CID) V8, automatic transmission, power windows and power brakes.

Maverick 2-Door Ford offered the 1974 Maverick as a no nonsense compact that was available in 3 models. Standard was a 3300cc (200CID) 6 and 3-speed manual transmission.

Gran Torino Brougham 2-Door Hardtop Ten models —four 2-door hard-tops, three 4-door Pillared hardtops and three wagons—made up the intermediate-size Ford Torino line in 1974. Standard was a 5000cc (302CID) V8 and 3-speed manual transmission.

Ford Thunderbird   Offered in coupe form, Ford's big T-Bird achieved a somewhat sleeker look for 1974. Standard was a 7200cc (460CID) V8, automatic transmission, air conditioning, power front disc brakes, power steering, power windows, steel-belted radial tires and radio. Sales of the 5100-lb, 102·4-inch wheelbase luxury 2-door dropped from nearly 80,000 in 1973 to 46,365 in 1974.

Mercury Montego MX Brougham   In 1974, a 5000cc (302CID) V8 became standard on all eight Montego models. A 7200cc (460CID) V8 was a popular option. Completing the intermediate class Montego line was a 2-door MX Brougham, 4-door and 2-door MX hardtop, a Sports Appearance sedan, 2-door and 4-door sedans and a wagon.

Lincoln-Mercury Comet GT   Although more elaborately trimmed, 1974 Mercury Comet 2-door and 4-door sedans shared basic style, wheelbases and drive train specifications with the Ford Division's Maverick. Standard was a 3300cc (200CID) 6 with 3-speed manual transmission. Optional were a 4100cc (250CID) V6 and 5000cc (302CID) V8. Sales of 82,565 Comet compacts made it Lincoln-Mercury's leading seller in 1974.

Cougar XR-7   The Lincoln-Mercury general manager, William P. Benton, is standing beside the all-new 1974 Cougar XR-7. Its redesigned features include new sheet-metal, new body/frame construction, new suspension, a Landau roof and opera window. Standard on the intermediate, 114-inch wheelbase, luxury coupe was a 5700cc (351CID) V8, automatic transmission, steel-belted radials, power brakes and power steering.

CHRYSLER CORPORATION

AMERICAN MOTORS CORPORATION

Dodge Dart Sport Coupe   Although nearly all Chrysler-Plymouth and Dodge lines lost volume in 1974, Chrysler's Plymouth Valiant and its clone, the Dodge Dart, were up with industry leaders in compact sales. Available in eight models, a 108-inch wheelbase sports coupe and 111-inch Dart 2-door and 4-door sedans, a 3300cc (198CID) 6, 3-speed manual transmission, torsion bar suspension and electronic ignition were standard. Dodge sold 232,848 Darts and Plymouth 337,585 Valiants in 1974.

AMC Matador 'X' Coupe   AMC's all-new Matador 'X' coupe was 4 inches shorter and over an inch lower than other Matador models. Standard for the 114-inch sporty 5 passenger 'X' 2-door was a 5000cc (304CID) V8. Matador sales, including Broughams, wagons and standard coupes reached 72,233 in 1974.

Plymouth Fury Gran Sedan 4-Door Hardtop   A lower beltline with increased glass area affording greater visibility were features in the new, 1974 Plymouth Fury. Standard for the Fury Gran 4-door, 2-door and Suburban wagon was Chrysler's 6600cc (400CID) V8. A 5700cc (360CID) V8 was standard on remaining models. Except for Fury wagons, which rode on the 124-inch wheelbase, a 122-inch wheelbase was standard.

AMC Gremlin   Although it was America's first subcompact, Gremlin sales—102,648 in 1974 and 133,018 in 1973—reflected AMC's lack of a 4-cylinder engine. Standard for the 1974, 96-inch wheelbase hatchback was a 3800cc (232CID) 6, 3-speed manual transmission and a new grille.

1975

US passenger car registrations fell to 7,448,921 in 1975, off 5·23 percent from 1974. Imports accounted for 1,500,928—18·17 percent of 1975's total sales.

All four American auto makers lost volume, although General Motors' share of the market increased slightly to 43·21 percent with Ford at 23·06 percent, Chrysler 11·70 and American Motors 3·72.

The automotive emission control law of 1972 was joined in late 1975 by a fuel economy act committing the industry to reducing fuel consumption by 40 percent, by 1980. Fleet averages, the combined city–highway miles-per-gallon achieved by a manufacturers's entire line, were to reach 18 mpg in 1978, 19 mpg in 1979 and 20 mpg in 1980.

Predictably, during a period of fuel shortages and rising costs, the V8 engine lost ground as economical 4s gained. However, although more than 80 percent of 1975s new cars were delivered with fuel-saving radial tires, 70 percent had air conditioning, an expensive and weight-robbing option.

During 1975, the 'bare bones', just under $2000 subcompact of 1970 reached $3000 as US manufacturers offered 57 different lines with over 300 models.

GENERAL MOTORS

Relatively soon after initiating its 'downsizing' program GM introduced a number of smaller, lighter 1975 models.

New were fuel-efficient V6 and smaller V8 engines. Standard equipment on all 1975 GM cars were high energy ignition systems compatible for use with unleaded fuel and catalytic converter emission control.

Chevrolet Monza 2+2 Available only as a 2-door hatchback in 1975, Chevy's 97-inch wheelbase subcompact Monza sports coupe was equipped with a 4-cylinder 2300cc (140CID) aluminum block engine and 4-speed manual transmission. Larger engines and automatic transmissions were options. Price from $4000, 113,946 Monzas were sold in 1975.

Chevrolet Nova LN 4-Door   Characterized by a greater glass area and a squared-off front end, Chevrolet's newly designed Nova came in 16 coupe and sedan models. Compact class, the 111-inch wheelbase Novas were equipped with a 4100cc (250CID) 6 and 3-speed manual transmissions. 4300cc (262CID) V8s were an additional $75.

Pontiac Astre 2-Door Hatchback   Pontiac entered the subcompact field in 1975 with the 97-inch wheelbase Astre. Standard was a 2300cc (140CID) overhead cam 4 and 3-speed manual transmission. Available as hatchback coupes and 2-door wagons with flush tailgates, close to 52,000 Astres were sold in 1975.

Chevrolet Blazer   Offered in both 2-wheel and 4-wheel drive, Blazer engines ranged from the 4100cc (250CID) 6 to large V8s. Chevy's entry in the popular recreational vehicle field, the 106·5-inch wheelbase Blazer, one of 6 utility sports models sold by GM in 1975, was available in both closed or open models.

Pontiac Grand Le Mans Colonnade Hardtop Coupe   Available as 112-inch wheelbase 2-door hardtops and 116-inch 4-door hardtops and estate wagons, Pontiac's intermediate class Le Mans was equipped with a 4100cc (250CID) 6 and, for the Safari wagon, a 6600cc (400CID) V8. Featured were new styling and reinforced fibreglass front-end panels.

Buick Electra LTD 4-Door Hardtop From 97-inch wheelbase, 2992-lb subcompact Skyhawks to 125-inch, 4800-lb Electras, illustrates the diversity of the Buick line. Buick sold over 3 times as many Electras as it did Skyhawks in a depressed 1975, which showed the optimism of American car buyers. Standard for the big Buick was a 7400cc (455CID) V8, power brakes, power windows, power steering and automatic transmission.

Cutlass Salon Colonnade Hardtop Coupe Standard on 112- and 116-inch wheelbase Cutlass intermediates, except for sedans and Vista estate wagons, which took 4300cc (260CID) and 5700cc (350CID) V8s and automatic transmissions, were a 4100cc (250CID) 6 and 3-speed manual transmission. Priced from $4000, Oldsmobile sold 324,610 of the 11 model Cutlass line in 1975.

Buick Skyhawk Hatchback Although differences between Chevy's Monza, Pontiac's Astre, Oldsmobile's Starfire and the Buick Skyhawk were largely matters of trim, Buick managed to add a touch of elegance, and a few dollars, to their version of GM's 97-inch wheelbase subcompact fastback. Standard for the 1975 Skyhawk was a 3800cc (231CID) V6 and 4-speed manual transmission.

Cadillac Seville Sedan When Cadillac introduced the 5-passenger, 4-door Seville in April, 1975, even sceptics accepted GM's downsizing program as more than hyperbole. About 25 inches shorter and 800 to 1000 lb lighter than other luxury sedans, the 114·3-inch wheelbase Seville's clean lines, luxury decor, advanced technology, and $12,500 price, created a class of its own. Seville standards were a 5700cc (350CID) electronically fuel-injected V8, automatic transmission, air conditioning and opulent interior appointments.

FORD MOTOR COMPANY

Granada 2-Door Sedan   All new in 1975, Granadas became Ford's biggest seller in their first year. Available as standard and Ghia 2-door and 4-door sedans, the 109·9-inch wheelbase intermediate came with a 3300cc (200CID) 6, solid state ignition, 3-speed manual transmission and steel-belted radial tires. A larger 6, V8s and automatic transmissions were popular options. Priced from $3750, 291,140 Granadas were bought in 1975.

Mercury Bobcat Runabout   New in 1975 was Lincoln-Mercury's version of Ford's popular Pinto. Using similar specs—94·5 and 94·8 inches for Runabout and wagon wheelbases, a 2300cc (140CID) 4 with 4-speed manual transmissions—and featuring slightly more elaborate trim, Bobcat options included sun roofs and aluminum wheels.

Elite 2-Door Hardtop   Also new in 1975 was Ford's 114-inch wheelbase Elite, a Thunderbird-type luxury entry in the intermediate field. Offered as a coupe only, standard Elite equipment included a 5800cc (351CID) V8 with solid state ignition, automatic transmission, power steering, power front disc brakes and steel-belted radial tires.

Ford LTD 4-Door Pillared Hardtop   Ford's 121-inch wheelbase, 4451-lb LTD line consisted of eight models, all trim variations of basic 2-door, 4-door and wagon models. Standard on the big Fords was a 5800cc (351CID) V8 (wagons used 6600cc (400CID) V8s), automatic transmission, power steering, power front disc brakes and steel-belted radial tires.

CHRYSLER CORPORATION

Cordoba Coupe Chrysler sold over 141,000 Cordobas, their all-new mid-size luxury coupe, during its first year. Available only as a 115-inch wheelbase 2-door, a 6600cc (400CID) V8 and an automatic transmission were standard for the $5400 Cordoba.

Mercury Capri II Made in West Germany by Ford of Europe and distributed in the US by Lincoln-Mercury, 1975 Capris were offered as 3-door hatchbacks. Standard on Ford's captive import was a 2300cc (140CID) 4, 4-speed manual transmission, rack and pinion steering and power assisted front disc brakes. Popular options were 2800cc (171CID) V6s and sun roof.

Dodge Ramcharger Made by Chrysler's Dodge division for the sports/utility market, Ramchargers came with either 2-wheel or 4-wheel drive, but not with both. Standard was a 3700cc (225CID) 6 or a 5200cc (318CID) V8. Properly equipped, 4-wheel drive Ramchargers towed up to 5000 lb. 2-wheel drive models with the 3700cc 6 were priced from $4000.

AMERICAN MOTORS CORPORATION

AMC Pacer Coupe Introduced in February, 1975, the short, squat, Pacer Coupe with 100-inch wheelbase, 171·5 inches overall, 77-inch wide, had extensive window area. Unique was the Pacer feature permitting rear seat passengers easy entry/exit by having kerb-side doors 4 inches longer than the driver's. Offered in three coupes, standard, sport 'X' and luxury D/L, a 3800cc (232CID) in-line 6 was standard. Priced from $3500, Pacer sales reached 96,769 in 1975.

Bricklin Young Malcolm Bricklin's car-building venture was an American success story gone haywire. Designed in Michigan with executive offices in Arizona, Bricklin's sleek, gull-wing sport coupe was built in New Brunswick, Canada. An entrepreneur who was said to have made his first million before reaching 30, Bricklin was better at signing-up dealers than making cars. Constructed of fibreglass and acrylics, the 96-inch wheelbase, 178·6 inches overall, 2-passenger fastback was originally powered by a 5900cc (360CID) American Motors V8, then a 5800cc (351CID) Ford V8. Equipped with air conditioning, AM/FM radio, alloy wheels, integral roll-cage, radial tires and a choice of automatic or 4-speed manual transmission, 2880 of the $10,000 Bricklin were made prior to filing for bankruptcy in December, 1975.

1976

Although gasoline was higher priced, it was relatively plentiful during 1976 and Americans responded by purchasing 9,751,485 new automobiles—a near record. Slowing slightly, the sale of 1,446,637 imports represented 14·83 percent of the US total. Dealers reported difficulty in keeping larger models in stock while subcompact sales sagged.

General Motors' share of the market increased to 47·22 percent. Counting only US-made cars raised GM's share to 57·76 per cent. Ford slipped to 22·45, Chrysler's share rose to 12·91 and American Motors fell to 2·53.

Prices held for most 1976 lines. The popularity of V8 engines rumbled back to 70 percent. Three out of 4 new cars sold during 1976 were air conditioned, and 92 percent had automatic transmissions.

GENERAL MOTORS

Chevrolet Impala Thirteen restyled Impala/Caprice models were offered in 1976. Standard on all but wagons, which took a 6600cc (400CID) V8, was a 5700cc (350CID) V8, automatic transmission, power brakes and power steering. 1976 sales of Chevrolet's largest line, 121·5-inch wheelbase, exceeded 454,000 units, up sharply from 1975.

Chevrolet Chevette Introduced in 1976, the 94·3-inch wheelbase, 2019-lb subcompact Chevette became America's smallest motorcar. Retaining a conventional front engine and rear wheel drive, Chevettes were offered as 2-passenger scooters and 4-passenger hatchbacks. Standard was GM's new 1400cc (85CID) 4 and 4-speed manual transmission. Popular options were a 1600cc (98CID) 4 and automatic transmission. Priced from $3000, 136,872 Chevettes were sold in 1976.

Pontiac Bonneville Brougham One of eight models in Pontiac's standard-size Bonneville/Catalina series, the Bonneville Brougham 4-door hardtop sedan came with a 6600cc (400CID) V8, automatic transmission, power brakes and power steering.

Pontiac Ventura Improved fuel economy and new front-end styling were 1976 Ventura features. Standard on Pontiac's 111·1-inch wheelbase compact was a 4100cc (250CID) 6 with optional 4300cc (260CID) and 5700cc (350CID) V8s. Available only with the 3800cc (231CID) V6 was a 5-speed manual transmission with overdrive 5th gear, a relative rarity on American cars in 1976. Two 4-door sedans, two hatchbacks and two 2-door coupes completed the $3600 to $4200 Ventura line.

Oldsmobile Omega Brougham Coupe New to Oldsmobile's compact-size, 111·2-inch wheelbase Omega line in 1976 was the Brougham 2-door. Standard on all 7 Omega models was a 4100cc (250CID) 6 and 3-speed manual transmission. Options included 4300cc (260CID) and 5700cc (350CID) V8s. Priced from $3600, Omega sales reached 54,806 in 1976.

Oldsmobile Delta 88 Hardtop Sedan Representing Olds in the intermediate category were 116-inch wheelbase Delta hardtop coupes, sedans and Custom Cruiser wagons. Standard for all but the wagon, which used a 7400cc (455CID) V8, was a 5700cc (350CID) V8, automatic transmission, power brakes, power windows and power steering. Priced from $5200, combined Delta and Custom Cruiser sales were 165,120 in 1976.

Buick Century Custom Sedan Buick's 112-inch wheelbase, mid-size, Century series was offered in four 2-door coupes, three 4-door sedans and, on 116-inch wheelbases, two estate wagons. Standard, except for the wagon's 5700cc (350CID) V8, was a 3800cc (231CID) V6 and automatic transmission. Priced from $4000, 1976 sales of 283,039 represented a sharp increase over 1975.

Cadillac Eldorado Convertible Pictured here is an endangered species, the last model of the only American-made convertible. Standard for the 126·3-inch wheelbase, 5100-lb, front-wheel-drive, $12,000 Eldorado was an 8200cc (500CID) V8, automatic transmission, air conditioning, AM/FM radio and steel-belted radial tires.

GMC Edgemont Motor Home Recreational vehicle sales rebounded in 1976 as fuel supplies improved. Makers of many vans and light pickup trucks, GMC also offered three 26-foot long models of mobile homes. Built on a low-frame chassis with aluminum and fibreglass bodies, the $25,500 Edgemont used a 7400cc (455CID) V8 with automatic transmission. Available in a variety of floor plans, the model shown had sleeping accommodation for 6 adults.

Plymouth Arrow Hatchback Built in Japan by Mitsubishi Motors, in whom Chrysler held a 15 percent interest, Plymouth's Arrow and Mitsubishi-made Dodge Colt subcompacts were available with a 1600cc (97·63CID) 4 and 4-speed manual transmission. Optional was a 2000cc (122CID) 4 and 5-speed manual transmission with overdrive. Priced from $3400, 168,296 Arrows and Colts were sold in 1976.

CHRYSLER CORPORATION

Dodge Aspen Custom Coupe The all-new, compact-size Dodge Aspen helped Chrysler sell a record 1,380,912 passenger cars in 1976. Available as a 112·5-inch wheelbase sedan and wagon and 108·5-inch coupe, Aspens were delivered with a 3700cc (225CID) 6 or, when ordered with optional automatic transmission, a 5200cc (318CID) or 5900cc (360CID) V8.

Plymouth Volare Station Wagon Volare, Plymouth's companion to the Dodge Aspen, also sold well during 1976, its introductory year. Standard on the 108·5-inch wheelbase coupe and 112·5-inch wagon and sedan was a 3700cc (225CID) 6 and 3-speed manual transmission. Automatic transmissions accompanied the optional 5200cc (318CID) V8. Priced from $3600, combined Volare/Aspen sales reached 504,091 in 1976.

AMERICAN MOTORS

Hornet Wagon Offered as a 2-door hatchback, a 2-door sedan, a 4-door sedan and a 4-door wagon, the 108-inch wheelbase Hornet series featured a new solid-state electronic ignition system. Standard was a 3800cc (232CID) 6. Options included a 4200cc (258CID) 6 and 5000cc (304CID) V8. Sales of 80,415 Hornets made it AMC's 1976 best seller.

FORD MOTOR COMPANY

Granada Ghia 4-Door Sedan Introduced in 1975, the 382,410 Granadas sold during 1976 made the 109.9-inch wheelbase compact Ford's most popular line. Available as 2-door and 4-door sedans with a 3300cc (200CID) 6 and 3-speed manual transmission, a 4100cc (250CID) 6 was standard for the Ghia coupe and sedan. Ghia options included 5000cc (302CID) and 5800cc (351CID) V8s and automatic transmission. 1976 prices ranged from $3700 for standard coupes to $4400 for Ghia sedans.

Mustang II Available in regular and Ghia models were fastback coupes with fold-down rear seats and 2-door coupes. Standard on the 96·2-inch wheelbase subcompact was a 2300cc (140CID) 4 with 4-speed manual transmission, rack and pinion steering and front disc brakes. Automatic transmissions were a $248 option, and a 2800cc (171CID) V6 was available on the Mach I fastback for $306.

Ford Pinto At $2900, the 94·5-inch subcompact Pinto fastback coupe was the lowest-priced car in Ford's 1976 line. Available on a marginally longer, 94·8-inch wheelbase, was a 3-door wagon. Standard was a 2300cc (140CID) 4, 4-speed manual transmission and rack and pinion steering. 1976 Pinto sales were 228,513.

1976

International Scout International Harvester's truck division built the first Scout, a popular recreational-suburbanite vehicle, in 1961. Available as either 2-wheel or 4-wheel-drive, the 1976 100-inch wheelbase Scout II was driven by a 5700cc (345CID) V8 or optional diesel, the first offered in its field. Capable of pulling trailers of up to 5000 lb, Scouts had 103 cubic feet of cargo space. 4-wheel-drive was offered in a dash-operated single-speed transfer case or floor-mounted 2-speed transfer case. Power disc brakes were standard. Options included automatic transmissions and air conditioning. Scout II, upper left, was participating in rugged Mexican Baja 500 off-road race.

1977

Americans bought 10,751,925 new cars in 1977, the second largest number ever registered in a single year. The sale of 1,967,759 imports raised their share of the market to 18·55 percent.

Both 4-cylinder and V6-engined American-made compacts and subcompacts lost ground. The use of V8s roared back to 77 percent. Eight of 10 new cars were air conditioned and 95·75 percent had automatic transmissions.

Until the last quarter, when sales slowed, dealers begged their factories for 'more big cars'. Full-size Chevrolets were 1977s best sellers.

At 46·37 and 22·61 percent, General Motors' and Ford's share of the market were little changed. Chrysler, with 10·98 percent, was off 1·93, a loss of 78,000 units. American Motors dropped to a 1·69 share of market.

New car costs increased around 6 percent. Two-tier pricing (promoting stripped, lower-priced models where import competition was most severe, such as in California) became commonplace.

GENERAL MOTORS

In 1977, 4 years and 1·1 billion dollars after starting their 'downsizing' program, GM introduced a line of redesigned full-size cars. Reduced in weight by 700 lb, and averaging 3 mpg better fuel consumption, GM succeeded in retaining ample interior dimensions on their new models while reducing their overall size and weight.

Chevrolet Caprice Landau Coupe   The 1977 Caprice/Impala, Chevy's 116-inch wheelbase 'big cars', fell within intermediate-size guide lines. Sold as a 2-door coupe, 4-door sedan and estate wagon, a 4100cc (250CID) 6 with automatic transmission was standard except for the wagon's 5000cc (305CID) V8. Priced from $4900, 1977 Caprice/Impala sales reached 628,253, tops for the industry.

Chevrolet Concours 4-Door Sedan   Offered as 111-inch wheelbase 2-door coupes, 4-door sedans and hatchback coupes, in Concours and basic lines, Nova prices ranged from $3500 for the coupe to $4200 for the Concours hatchback. Standard was the 4100cc (250CID) 6 and 3-speed manual transmission. Popular options were automatic transmissions and a range of larger V8s. Chevy dealers sold 303,000 Novas in 1977.

Chevrolet Fleetside Pickup   Total RV (recreational vehicles include vans, campers, motor homes and pickup trucks) sales reached a near-record 745,600 in 1977 as light pickups became widely used for personal transportation. Offered on a 131·5-inch wheelbase with both 2-wheel and 4-wheel drive, the C-10 had a 1990 lb payload. Priced at $4308, a 4100cc (250CID) 6 was standard. An additional $185 made the 5000cc (305CID) V8 a popular option.

Pontiac Special Edition Trans Am Restyled for 1977, all four Firebird Sports coupes, the basic Firebird, Esprit, Formula and Trans Am, shared a 108·1-inch wheelbase. Engines ranged from a 3800cc (231 CID) V6 to the 6600cc (400CID) V8, which was standard on the Trans Am. Prices ranged from $4300 for the basic Firebird to $5500 for the Trans Am.

Pontiac Grand Prix SJ Coupe The $5742 SJ hardtop was one of three Grand Prix models, all coupes, that sold 234,629 units, tops for the 1977 Pontiac line. Standard on the 116-inch wheelbase coupe (1978 Grand Prix would use a 108·1-inch wheelbase) was a 5000cc (301 CID) V8, automatic transmission, power brakes and power steering.

Cutlass 2-Door Colonnade Hardtop Coupe Featuring a newly-designed front-end and fastback rear deck, 1977 Cutlass 4-door sedans were on 116-inch wheelbases, while 2-door coupes used 112 inches. Standard was a 3800cc (231CID) V8, 3-speed manual transmission, power steering and power brakes. Optional were V8s of 4300cc (260CID), 5700cc (350CID), 6600cc (403CID) and 5-speed manual or automatic transmissions. Priced from $4400 to $5300, over 480,000 of the Cutlass line were sold in 1977.

Buick Regal Coupe Available as a 112-inch wheelbase 2-door and 116-inch 4-door, the 1977 Regal Coupe was sold with a 3800cc (231CID) V6 and 3-speed manual transmission. A 5700cc (350CID) V8 and automatic transmission was standard on the sedan. Both the $4700 coupe and $5300 sedan came with power steering and brakes. Buick discontinued the sedan in 1978 when they reduced the coupe's wheelbase to 108·1 inches.

Oldsmobile Toronado Brougham Restyled for 1977, Old's front-wheel-drive 2-door featured a new electronic system using on-board digital computers that adjusted ignition timing for optimum driveability and emissions control. Priced from $8200, the 122-inch wheelbase, standard-size coupe was delivered with a 6600cc (403CID) V8, automatic transmission and air conditioning.

Buick Skyhawk Buick's 97-inch wheelbase subcompact was equipped with a 3800cc (231CID) V6 and 4-speed manual transmission. Automatic and 5-speed manual transmissions were $248 options. Two coupes, a $4000 fastback and $4300 hatchback, were offered.

FORD MOTOR COMPANY

Buick Opel Standard Coupe   Unfavourable exchange rates resulted in 1977 Opels being made by Isuzu Motors in Japan rather than by GM in West Germany. An 1800cc (111CID) 4, 4-speed manual transmission and power brakes were standard on the $3400, and up, 94·3-inch wheelbase subcompact.

Pinto Wagon   Standard for the 94·8-inch subcompact Pinto wagon was a 2300cc (140CID) 4, 4-speed manual transmission, rack and pinion steering and front disc brakes. Options included a 2800cc (170·8CID) V6 and automatic transmission. 1977 Pinto sales were 211,656 of which 77,320 were wagons.

Cadillac Seville   Changes in the 1977 Seville sedan were a new grille and the addition of 4-wheel disc brakes as standard equipment. Also standard was a 5700cc (350CID) fuel-injected V8, automatic transmission, air conditioning and full complement of power assists. At $13,400, the 114·3-inch wheelbase, 4300 lb Seville was Cadillac's smallest and, except for their limousines, most costly model.

King Cobra Mustang II   Originally built by Carroll Shelby as sports racing cars using Ford V8s, Cobras dominated US road-racing in the mid-60s, and Shelby played key roles in Ford's GT-40 and MkII programs which four times won Le Mans. Unlike other 1977 Mustang II's, King Cobras were driven by 5000cc (302CID) V8s. Built on the 96·2-inch Mustang II wheelbase, King Cobras were priced from $4500.

CHRYSLER CORPORATION

Dodge B200 Custom Van   Delivered with suggestions for painting a variety of striking exterior designs and with templates for adding portholes and sun roofs, individualizing your van to reflect your personality was what being one of the van clan was all about. Available on a 109 or 127-inch wheelbase with a 3700cc (225CID) 6 for $4350 or 5200cc (318CID) V8 at $4500, Dodge vans were capable of 2800 lb payloads.

AMERICAN MOTORS

Dodge Diplomat   Introduced in May, 1977, the all-new Dodge Diplomat was offered as a 2-door coupe and 4-door sedan. Standard for the 112·7-inch wheelbase intermediate was a 5200cc (318CID) V8 with automatic transmission. Priced from $4900, 34,360 Diplomats were built in 1977.

Pacer Station Wagon   New in 1977 was AMC's 2-door, 4-passenger estate wagon. A 3800cc (232CID) in-line 6 and 3-speed manual transmission were standard on the 100-inch wheelbase, 174 inches overall Pacer. Options included a 3800cc (232CID) 6 and, for an additional $279, automatic transmission. Priced from $4000, 25,380 Pacer Wagons were sold in 1977.

Jeep CJ-5, CJ-7 and Cherokee Chief Made by Willys-Overland during World War II, then by Kaiser-Willys until acquired by AMC in 1970, the ubiquitous Jeep started America's love affair with 4-wheel-drive sports/utility vehicles. In addition to relatively stark CJ models, by 1977 there were 2-door and 4-door Cherokee wagons, a 4-door Wagoneer and pickup trucks. Standard on the 83·5-inch wheelbase CJ-5 and 93·5-inch CJ-7 were 4-wheel-drive, a 3800cc (232CID) 6 and 3-speed manual transmission. Automatic or 4-speed manual transmissions, a 4200cc (258CID) 6 and 5000cc (304CID) V8 were options. Cherokee specifications show a 108·7-inch wheelbase, 4-wheel-drive, 4200cc (258CID) 6, 3-speed manual transmission and power front disc brakes as standard. Priced from $5000 to $8000, 132,679 Jeeps were sold in 1977.

1978

New car registrations reached 10,946,104, a 2·23 percent increase over 1977 and the nation's third best year.

Imports accounted for 1,946,094 of 1978s new car sales for a 17·78 percent share of the US total.

Subcompacts increased in popularity; compacts retained their share, while sales of intermediates and standard models declined.

Prices rose about 5 percent, and 66 percent of 1978s automobiles used a V8 engine.

General Motors' share of the market rose to 47·67 percent, 57·86 not counting imports. Ford stayed near 23 percent as Chrysler declined to 10·16 and American Motors slipped to 1·44.

A major auto maker joined the American establishment during 1978 when Volkswagen opened its Pennsylvania plant.

GENERAL MOTORS

GM carried their 'downsizing' program into 1978 by cutting pounds and inches from its intermediate models while retaining passenger space and improving fuel consumption by an average of 3 mpg. New engines, 4s, V6s, a big V8 diesel and, selectively, turbocharging, became GM realities. Also a reality, 1978 saw GM drop their ill-starred Vega.

Chevrolet Monte Carlo   All-new 1978 Monte Carlo coupes were 800 lb lighter and a foot shorter than previous models. Standard for the 108·1-inch wheelbase, 200·4 inches overall, compact was a 3800cc (231 CID) V6 with a 3-speed manual transmission. Priced from $4800 for the Sport coupe to $5700 for the Landau, on which the automatic transmission was standard, 1978 Monte Carlo sales reached 348,751.

Chevrolet El Camino Pickup   Redesigned for 1978, Chevy's El Camino luxury pickup was a foot shorter and 599 lb lighter than former models, but it still carried 800-lb cargoes and pulled 5000-lb trailers. Available with a 3300cc (200 CID) V6, a 5700cc (350 CID) V8 was standard in higher altitudes. 1978 El Camino sales were 53,437.

Pontiac Grand Am 4-Door Sedan   Discontinued after 1975, the Grand Am returned in 1978 on a 108·1-inch wheelbase with a 4900cc (301 CID) V8, automatic transmission, power brakes and power steering as standard. RTS (Rally Tuned Suspension) also was standard on the $5500 Grand Am coupe and $5600 sedan.

Oldsmobile Starfire Sport Coupe   The 97-inch wheelbase subcompact Starfire was available with a 2500cc (151CID) 4 and 4-speed manual transmission. GM's 3800cc (231CID) V6 was a $170 option. Olds dealers sold fewer than 20,000 of the $4300 hatchback in 1978.

Cadillac Eldorado   Front-wheel-drive Eldorados came with a 5700cc (350CID) V8, air conditioning, electronic level control, power door locks, 4-wheel disc brakes and, of course, automatic transmission. 43,681 of the 113·9-inch wheelbase (shortest of all Cadillacs) $12,000 coupes were sold in 1978.

Buick LeSabre Sport Coupe   Buick's 115·9-inch wheelbase, 6-passenger LeSabre was one of the first American cars equipped with a turbocharged engine. Standard was a 3800cc (231CID) V6, automatic transmission, power brakes and power steering. Priced from $5400 for the basic coupe to $6300 for turbocharged sport coupes, 161,574 LeSabres were sold in 1978.

Chevrolet Corvette   Twenty-five years old in 1978, Corvettes remained America's only production sports car. 185·2 inches overall on a 98-inch wheelbase, the fibreglass-bodied coupe weighed 3503 lb. Standard was a 5700cc (350CID) V8 with 4-speed manual or automatic transmission. The high performance L-82, also a 5700cc (350CID) V8, was a popular $525 option. In 1978, the year Indianapolis used Corvettes as pace cars, Chevy dealers sold 40,426 of their $10,500, oversexed 2-seaters.

FORD MOTOR COMPANY

Not since 1960 when Ford introduced the Falcon as an import fighter and sold 417,174 during its first year, had Ford launched so successful a model as the Fairmont/Zepher.

Ford's Maverick and the Lincoln-Mercury Comet were discontinued. 1978 also was the first full year of Ford's 'world car', the subcompact Fiesta.

Fairmont/Futura New for 1978 was Ford's 105·5-inch wheelbase Fairmont (left). Available as 2-door and 4-door sedans and a 4-door wagon, a 2300cc (140CID) 4 with manual transmission was standard. Automatic transmission, a 3300cc (200CID) 6 and 5000cc (302CID) V8 were options. Priced from $3600 to $4100, Ford sold 399,995 Fairmonts in 1978.

Complementing the Fairmont was the Futura (above), a parallel line of more elaborately trimmed, more costly, Fairmont-based models.

Ford Fiesta Ford's new import, the 90-inch wheelbase subcompact Fiesta hatchback, used contemporary engineering concepts such as front-wheel-drive, transverse (sideways) mounted engines with 5-speed manual overdrive and aluminum-cased transaxles. Standard was a 1600cc (98CID) 4 with 2-barrelled Weber carburetor, rack and pinion steering, steel-belted radial tires and front-wheel discs. Offered in 4 states of trim, 76,001 of the $4400 Fiesta were sold in 1978.

Mercury Marquis 4-Door Pillared Hardtop Providing space for 6 passengers and 22·7 cubic feet for luggage, the 124-inch wheelbase Marquis provided big car comfort in the medium-price field. Standard were 5800cc (351CID) V8s, automatic transmission, power brakes, steering and windows. Offered in eight models, 1978 Marquis were priced from $5800 to $7300.

Ford LTD II 4-Door While retaining the 121-inch wheelbase for its LTD, Ford reduced the 1978 LTD II 2-door to 114 inches and the 4-door sedan to 118 but still provided room for 6 passengers. Standard were a 5000cc (302CID) V8, automatic transmission, power brakes and power steering. Priced from $5500, Ford sold 139,309 LTD IIs in 1978.

Zepher Z-7 Coupe Unlike the squared-off backs of Fairmont/Zepher sedans, Lincoln-Mercury's Z-7 had a sloping rear window and deck that was promoted as having an 'American look'! Sharing the 105·5-inch Zepher wheelbase, the Z-7 was 2 inches longer overall than regular Zephers. Standard was a 2300cc (140CID) 4; a 3300cc (200CID) 6 and 5000cc (302CID) V8 were options. Priced from $3800, over 120,000 of all Zepher models were sold in 1978.

CHRYSLER CORPORATION

Plymouth Sapporo/Dodge Challenger   Made for Chrysler by Mitsubishi of Japan, the new 99-inch wheelbase Plymouth Sapporo/Dodge Challenger 2-door was equipped with a 1600cc (98CID) 4, 5-speed manual transmission and power front disc brakes. A 2000cc (158CID) 4 was optional. 32,664 of the $5800 Sapporo/Challenger subcompacts were sold in 1978.

Dodge Omni/Plymouth Horizon   Early in 1976 Chrysler announced the first American-made front-wheel-drive subcompact and that it would use a transverse-mounted 1700cc (104·7CID) overhead cam 4 purchased from Volkswagen! Introduced in December 1977 as a 99·2-inch wheelbase, 4-door sedan, a 96·7-inch hatchback followed. Priced from $3800, 1978 sales of 113,081 Horizons and 84,081 Omnis appeared limited by the availability of engines.

AMERICAN MOTORS

Concord Hatchback   Introduced in 1978 as a replacement for the Hornet, AMC's 108-inch compact Concord was available as 2-door and 4-door sedans, a 4-door estate wagon and a hatchback coupe. Driven by a 1984cc (121CID) 4, a 4200cc (258CID) 6 or a 5000cc (304CID) V8, automatic transmissions were optional. Priced from $3900, 110,938 Concords were sold in 1978.

VOLKSWAGON OF AMERICA

Rabbit 4-Door Sedan   The first US-made Rabbit, Europe's Golf, rolled out of VW's Pennsylvania plant in April, 1978. Offered as 2-door and 4-door sedans, the 94·4-inch wheelbase, front-wheel-drive subcompact was driven by an imported 1500cc (88·9CID) overhead cam 4 and transaxle. Priced from $4700, options would include 5-speed and automatic transmissions, diesel engines and sun roofs.

1979

Americans purchased 10,334,911 new cars in 1979. Following a strong first quarter, 1979 sales of US-made autos fell to 7,995,907, a million less than in 1978. Consequently, although total US sales passed the ten-million mark, domestic sales were their poorest since 1975.

Imports, primarily those from Japan, accounted for 2,339,004 of the 1979 total, a record-shattering 22·63 percent of the US market.

Gasoline station queues returned in the spring of 1979. When both fuel and car costs soared, American motorists again reacted by choosing smaller cars. Intermediates lost 23·4 percent of their share of the market, and standard size cars fell 16·62. Subcompacts gained 15 as compact sales rose 1·36. The use of V8 engines declined to 58 percent.

General Motors' percentage of the total US market slipped to 46·48. Based on US-made cars only, GM's share was an awesome 60·39 percent. Ford and Chrysler dropped to 20·30 and 9·03 percent, and Volkswagon of America, with 2·01 percent, became the nation's 4th largest car maker, passing American Motors, whose share of the market was 1·95 percent.

GENERAL MOTORS

The 1979 model year saw GM drop the Chevrolet Nova and introduce a redesigned front-wheel-drive Oldsmobile Toronado, Buick Riviera and Cadillac Eldorado. Following a 5-year, 1·7 billion dollar retooling program, in April 1979, GM unveiled their advanced 'X' cars, the front-wheel-drive Chevrolet Citation, Pontiac Phoenix, Buick Skylark and Oldsmobile Omega. Over 800 lb lighter, with roomier interiors and better fuel economy than the models they replaced, the success of GM's 'X' line encouraged the whole of US industry.

Chevrolet Chevette Except for minor sheet metal alterations, slightly larger engines and a 25 percent increase in price, Chevy's Chevette remained unchanged since its 1975 introduction. Standard on the 94·3-inch wheelbase hatchback 2-door or 97·3-inch sedan was a 1600cc (98CID) 4 and 4-speed manual transmission. Automatic transmissions were a popular $320 option. America's best-selling subcompact, 363,216 of the $4000, and up, Chevettes were sold in 1979.

Chevrolet Camaro Berlinetta   New in 1979, the Berlinetta joined the standard Camaro, Rally Sport and high-performance Z-28. Chevy's 108-inch wheelbase, 197 inches overall, 3500-lb fastback had long been America's favourite 'street racer'. Standard on all but the Z-28, which came with Chevy's largest V8, was a 4100cc (250CID) 6. Optional were 5000cc (305CID) and 5700cc (350CID) V8s. Priced from $4800 to $6200, 203,627 Camaros were bought in 1979.

Chevrolet Citation   Introduced with justified fanfare in April 1979, a notch-back coupe, and 2-door and 4-door hatchback sedans made up the Citation line. Featuring front-wheel-drive, lightweight manual and automatic transaxles, front discs with dual braking systems and rack and pinion steering, the compact, 104·9-inch wheelbase, 176·7 inches overall, Citation came with a 2500cc (151CID) 4 and 4-speed manual transmission. A 2800cc (173CID) V6 and automatic transmission were optional. Priced from $4800, and in perennial short supply, over 290,000 Citations were sold in 1979.

Pontiac Formula Firebird   New front-end and rear deck treatments were features of all four 1979 Firebirds—basic, Esprit, Formula and Trans Am. A 4900cc (301CID) double-barrelled V8 and automatic transmission were standard on Formula models. Priced from $5200, 149,995 Firebirds were sold in 1979.

Pontiac Phoenix Pontiac's version of GM's 'X' car used the basic 109·9-inch wheelbase and the same transverse-mounted 2500cc (151CID) 4 or optional 2800cc (173CID) V6 as the Citation. Where the Phoenix and other 'X' models differed was in trim and minor, 2 to 5-inch variations, in overall length. The 5-door hatchback shown, was Pontiac's most popular 'X' car.

Oldsmobile Toronado Diesel power and front-wheel-drive, two relatively unusual features, distinguished GM's 1979 Toronado. Standard on the 114-inch 2-door Brougham, the single model offered, was a 5700cc (350CID) V8, automatic transmission, air conditioning, power brakes, power steering, power windows, power door locks and radio! The 5700cc (350CID) diesel was a $785 option. 45,348 of the $10,500 coupe were bought in 1979.

Oldsmobile Custom Cruiser Standard on this large, 116-inch wheelbase, 219·4 inches overall, 4100-lb estate wagon was a 5700cc (350CID) V8, automatic transmission, power brakes and power steering. A third seat and a 5700cc (350CID) V8 diesel were options. In 1979 Oldsmobile sold 27,052 of their $6900 wagons.

Oldsmobile Omega More than 18 inches shorter and 750 lb lighter than the model it replaced, the Omega, Oldsmobile's version of GM's 'X' car, was available as basic or deluxe 2-door and 4-door sedans. Introduced in April 1979 with a transverse-mounted 2500cc (151CID) 4 and 4-speed manual transmission, a 2800cc (173CID) V6 was a $225 option.

Buick Electra Park Avenue Sedan Buick's big—118-inch wheelbase, 222 inches overall, 4000 lb—Electra was offered in five models. Standard was a 5700 cc (350CID) V8 and automatic transmission. A 6600cc (403CID) V8 was a $70 option.

Buick Riviera Shorter, lighter and more fuel efficient, the 1979 Riviera was one of GM's large cars with F-W-D. Available as a 114-inch wheelbase 2-door, a 5700cc (350CID) V8, automatic transmission, power steering, power brakes and stereo were standard. A turbocharged 3800cc (231CID) V6 was available for $110, except on the 'S' coupe, where it was standard equipment. Over 49,500 of the $10,500 coupes were registered in 1979, which was double the number sold in 1978.

Cadillac Eldorado For 1979 GM's ultimate 'Personal' car, the F-W-D Cadillac Eldorado, shed 1200 lb as it shrank to a 113·9-inch wheelbase and 204 inches overall. Driven by a fuel-injected 5700cc (350CID) V8, standard equipment included almost every possible option except leather upholstery and diesel engines. 43,681 of the $14,500 Eldorado were bought in 1979.

FORD MOTOR COMPANY

Ford 2-Door Mustang   Completely new for 1979, the 4-place Mustang came as a 100·4-inch wheelbase 2-door coupe and 3-door hatchback. Standard was a 2300cc (140CID) overhead cam 4, 4-speed manual transmission and rack and pinion steering. Ghia and Cobra models included special trim and, standard on the Cobra, a 2300cc (140CID) turbocharged engine and heavy-duty stabilizer bars. Sales of 294,904 made the $4600 Mustang Ford's best seller in 1979.

Ford Granada   More than 1,000,000 Granadas were bought since its introduction in 1975. Offered in 3 lines, standard, Ghia and ESS, the 109·9-inch wheelbase compact was available as 2-door and 4-door sedans. A 4100cc (250CID) 6 with 4-speed manual transmission was standard. Automatic transmission and a 5000cc (302CID) V8 were popular options. Priced from $4500 to $5100, 141,116 Granadas were sold in 1979.

Ford LTD Country Squire Wagon   New in 1979, Ford's Country Squire wagon carried 6, or with optional facing rear seats, 8 passengers. Featuring Ford's 3-way tailgate, the 114·3-inch wheelbase, 214·7-inch overall wagon had 91·7 cubic feet of cargo capacity. Priced from $6950, a 5800cc (351CID) V8, automatic transmission, power steering and power brakes were standard.

Mercury Capri   Discontinued in 1977 when unfavourable currency exchange made the German-built captive import non-competitive, Ford introduced a US-built Capri 3-door liftback as the Lincoln-Mercury division's example of the new Mustang, using the same 100·4-inch wheelbase and 2300cc (140CID) overhead cam 4. Optional were an AiResearch TO-3 turbocharger, sport and Rally suspensions, a 2800cc (171CID) V6 and 5000cc (302CID) V8. Priced from $4600, 88,404 Capris were bought in 1979.

Lincoln-Mercury Bobcat Restyled for the first time since its 1975 debut, the 94·5-inch wheelbase subcompact boasted a new grille, sloping hood and rectangular headlights. Available as a 3-door liftback and 2-door estate wagon, a 2300cc (140CID) 4 and manual transmission were standard. Sales of the $3900 Bobcat increased to 43,032 in 1979.

Lincoln Versailles Introduced in April 1977, as Ford's reply to GM's Cadillac Seville, the compact Lincoln Versailles used the 109·9-inch Ford Granada wheelbase. Driven by an electronically controlled 5000cc (302CID) V8, standard were automatic transmission, air conditioning, 4-wheel power disc brakes, power windows, power steering, AM/FM stereo and a vinyl roof. Sales of the luxurious, $13,500 4-door were 13,511 in 1979. Following the 1980 model run, the Versailles was discontinued.

CHRYSLER CORPORATION

Plymouth Champ   The Plymouth Champ hatchback was one of five cars (Dodge, Colt and Challenger; Plymouth Arrow and Sapporo are the others) made by Mitsubishi of Japan. Standard on the front-wheel-drive, 90·6-inch wheelbase subcompact was a transverse-mounted 1400cc (86CID) 4, a 4-speed manual transmission and power disc brakes. A $4600 custom hatchback with a 1600cc (97·5CID) 4 and automatic transmission was also available.

New Yorker Fifth Avenue   Top of the Chrysler line and, at 221·5 inches overall, the longest, by a fraction of an inch, of all 1979 motorcars, the 3920-lb New Yorker was offered only as a 4-door sedan. Standard was a 5900cc (360CID) V8, automatic transmission, power brakes and power windows. 32,650 of the $8900 New Yorkers were sold in 1979.

AMERICAN MOTORS

October 1979 saw Renault acquire a 5 percent interest in American Motors. Subsequent reports indicate that the French firm planned to become AMC's largest stockholder by increasing their share to 22·5 percent. In addition to cooperating on technical matters, AMC dealers now handle selected Renault models in the US while Renault has European sales rights to AMC's Jeep.

AMC Spirit Liftback   First to drive AMC's new subcompact Spirit were residents of Spirit, Wisconsin, a village of 350 inhabitants. Replacing AMC's discontinued Gremlin, the 96-inch wheelbase Spirit was available as a 2-door sedan and 2-door liftback. Standard was a 2000cc (121CID) 4 and 4-speed manual transmission. Optional were larger engines and automatic transmission. Priced from $4000, 53,429 Spirits were sold in 1979.

MAJOR AMERICAN CARS: 1970–1979

American Motors Corporation

Ambassador 10, 27
Concord 55
Gremlin 14, 18, 27, 32
Hornet 10, 19, 27, 43
Javelin 14
Jeep 50
Matador 14, 27, 32
Pacer 38, 49
Spirit 62

Chrysler Corporation

Cordoba 37
Le Baron 13
New Yorker 62
Newport 19
Plymouth Arrow 42
Champ 62
Cricket 26
Fury 13, 32
Horizon 55
Sapporo 55
Sebring 19
Valiant 8
Volare 42
Dodge Aspen 42
Camper 9
Challenger 55
Charger 9
Club Cab 26
Colt 26
Coronet 20
Custom Van 9, 49
Dart 14, 32
Diplomat 49
Omni 55
Ramcharger 37

Ford Motor Company

Ford Division
Elite 36
Fairmont 53
Fiesta 54
Ford 8, 25, 36, 54, 60
Futura 53
Granada 36, 43, 60
Maverick 13, 30
Mustang 7, 17, 43, 48, 60
Pinto 12, 24, 43, 48
Thunderbird 17, 31
Torino 7, 17, 30
Lincoln-Mercury Division Ford
Motor Company
Bobcat 36, 61
Capri 24, 37, 60
Comet 31
Cougar 18, 31
Cyclone 8
Lincoln 8, 18, 61
Marquis 13, 24, 54
Montego 17, 31
Zepher 54

General Motors Corporation

Buick Apollo 29
Century 41
Electra 7, 16, 35, 59
Le Sabre 12, 52
Regal 23, 47
Riviera 6, 29, 59
Skyhawk 35, 47
Cadillac Calais 16
Coupe de Ville 23
Eldorado 12, 41, 52, 59
Fleetwood 7, 30
Sedan de Ville 12
Seville 35, 48
Chevrolet Blazer 34
Camaro 57
Caprice 11, 45
Chevelle 5, 22
Chevette 39, 56
Citation 57
Concours 45
Corvette 52
El Camino 51
Fleetside 45
Impala 39
Kingswood 15
Malibu 15
Monte Carlo 5, 28, 51
Monza 33
Nova 11, 34
Vega 10, 21
Oldsmobile Custom Cruiser
Cutlass 6, 16, 29, 35, 47
88 16, 41
98 6, 22
Omega 23, 29, 40, 59
Starfire 52
Toronado 12, 47, 58
Pontiac Astre 34
Bonneville 40
Catalina 5
Firebird 28, 57
Grand Am 51
Grand Prix 6, 15, 28, 46
Grand Ville 11, 22
GTO 11
Le Mans 34
Phoenix 58
Trans Am 46
Ventura 22, 40
GMC Motor Home 42

Other Makes:

Bricklin 38
International Scout 44
Opel 23, 48
Volkswagon of America,
   Rabbit 55